Finding Hope in the Darkness of Grief

Spiritual Insights Expressed through Art, Poetry and Prose

By Diamante Lavendar

Interior Graphics/Art Credit: Diamante Lavendar

Balboa Press books may be ordered through booksellers or by contacting:

Balboa Press
A Division of Hay House
1663 Liberty Drive
Bloomington, IN 47403
www.balboapress.com
1 (877) 407-4847

Because of the dynamic nature of the Internet, any web addresses or links contained in this book may have changed since publication and may no longer be valid. The views expressed in this work are solely those of the author and do not necessarily reflect the views of the publisher, and the publisher hereby disclaims any responsibility for them.

Any people depicted in stock imagery provided by Getty Images are models, and such images are being used for illustrative purposes only.
Certain stock imagery © Getty Images.

ISBN: 978-1-9822-0568-3 (sc)
ISBN: 978-1-9822-0569-0 (e)

Print information available on the last page.

Balboa Press rev. date: 06/04/2018

BALBOA
PRESS
A DIVISION OF HAY HOUSE

Dedication

To my children who wait for me
beyond heaven's veil. I love you, I miss you,
and I have regrets. But I also have the hope
of seeing you again.

Dearest Celby and Jazzy, you blessed me
more than words can say.
You've taught me so much about love
and life. Most importantly, you've shown me
that this life, although fleeting, is not all there is.
There is so much more to appreciate and comprehend
beyond this dimension known as earth.

Foreword

This three-dimensional plane offers much for us to learn: happiness, wisdom, understanding, pain, loss, heartbreak, wonder, and enlightenment. It is a Pandora's box of emotions, situations, opportunities, and failures, all wrapped into a package we call life. Nobody is immune. But everybody has the opportunity to grow tall in this place of experience or to wither like a flower exposed to harsh sunlight. It's completely up to us as to how we choose to respond.

Finding Hope In The Darkness Of Grief is a gleaning of some of my own insights. It's been a long, difficult road, but it has taught me a lot of poignant lessons.

The art that I'm sharing can be found on my art site at www.diamante-lavendar.pixels.com . My quotes are available there as well. If some of my work resonates with you, I would consider it an honor for you to visit my site. If I can help others heal as I, myself, heal, then my work as an author and artist will have been well spent.

Even during the times you feel most alone,
there is always a presence watching you,
hearing your internal dialogue.
Don't be afraid. Don't feel alone.
Let the light lead you.

Understanding of Spirit

It hurts so much
To lose someone or something
That gives life joy and meaning.

It is so difficult
To be in a situation
Where peace eludes you at every turn.

It is heartbreaking
To be overcome with guilt, worry, and shame
Over situations in which you thought you failed.

But every hardship has a reason,
And every deprivation a purpose,
If you look through eyes of insight.

There is so much more
To every instance
Than we can comprehend.

Only Spirit, in its infinite wisdom,
Truly understands.
So we must make up our minds

To live in trust, no matter what we see with our natural eyes,
Because Spirit can create beauty from debilitation
And strength from desolation

If we trust that the Spirit of life understands
What is right for us
And has our best interests at heart.

In the dark night of the soul,
it is a tremendous help to know
that you aren't alone.
Negativity wants to twist your thinking
and make you believe
that no one else can understand your pain.
This is a dangerous deception.
It prompts you to believe in the illusion of separation
rather than the truth of togetherness.

In the illusion of separation,
you believe that you are the only one suffering.
You trust the mistruth that
nobody could ever understand
and that there is no way out.
Follow your heart. It wants you to find others
who can relate. And if you give it a chance,
you will find them, and they will help you heal.

False Beliefs

False beliefs crush
Even the most dedicated of people;

They are lies and burdens
To the spirit of a human being.

Things like distrust, anger, resentment,
Paranoia, anxiety, and depression:

They wound even the strongest soul;
They disrupt even the deepest serenity.

To live in peace does not mean
To ignore all that ails you.

To live in peace means to observe and to lay aside
These false beliefs and assumptions.

Look to those who have traveled before you
For wisdom and insight;

They will assist in pointing the way
Toward the path of introspection and contemplation—

The only road that leads
To genuine peace and happiness.

Healing is a lifelong commitment

That happens in layers;

From the outermost layer of the soul

To the innermost layer.

It is a process

That takes time and patience;

A process that must not be rushed.

-Diamante Lavendar

Scars mar the beauty of the maps of our lives. We all have scars.
If we embrace them and choose to learn from them,
they will make our lives more interesting, and they will gift us with deeper perception.
In some ways, scars make us more beautiful, because they create empathy within us.
Through the infliction of our own scars, we are given wisdom as to how to
help others deal with the scars they bear.

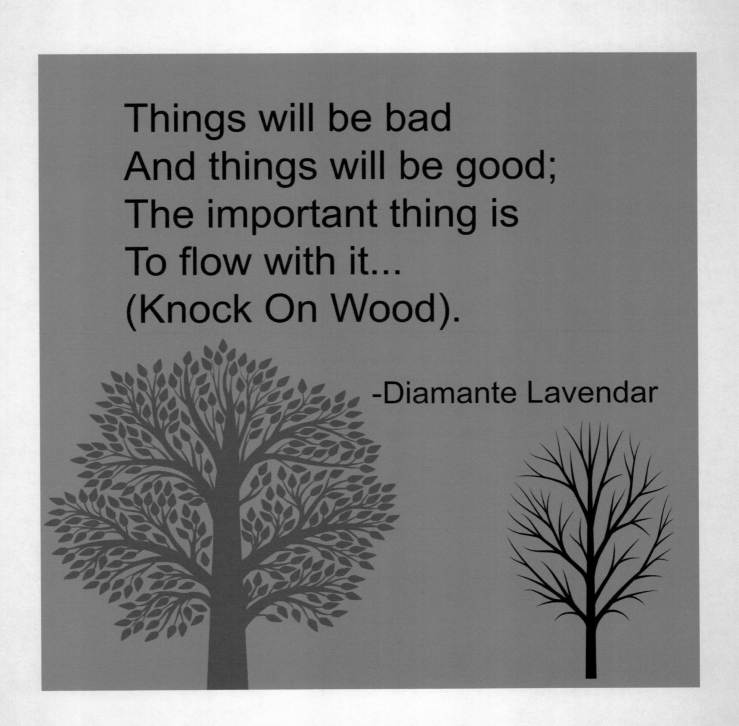

Things will be bad
And things will be good;
The important thing is
To flow with it...
(Knock On Wood).

-Diamante Lavendar

Life is in a constant state of flux. There will be good times
and there will be bad times.
To deny either is to deny the existence of this three-dimensional experience.
What you need to remember is that the definitions of *bad* and *good*
can get you in trouble.
Those labels cause preconceived notions, which in turn
lead to assumptions. Assumptions are not
based on spiritual truth.

Grief comes in many forms.
The most obvious is death. Other forms of grief
include abuse, loss, and difficult life changes, such as divorce.
While these experiences are heart-wrenching, they are also life-changing.
Spirit's great wisdom uses all forms of teaching to expand us
and to create depth within us.
While grief is not fun to deal with, it is a valuable tool
to bring about amazing change and growth. The key to this deep level of learning
is attitude. How will you respond to the pain you're feeling?

Guilt, like revenge and anger, is a negative emotion. Anything negative brings you down. You can feel it. You have the sensation of your heart sinking, of your dreams dying.

That is not what Spirit wants for you. And that is not what you should want for yourself.

In order to reach the beautiful heights available to you, you have to retain your focus. Keep your focus on love so you can keep evolving into the beautiful being of light that you were meant to be.

You Shone Like the Sun on Autumn Leaves

You shone like the sun on autumn leaves,

Their remaining life brief before they fell from the trees.

The sun's light was strong, the warmth intense,

Just as your heart: loving, immense.

But the leaves shriveled up and neared their end,

Just as you when you left, my child, my friend.

Your meaning lives on in every new day;

I begged God for time to extend your stay.

It's a hard lesson to learn that you have no control

Over life, over love, over a darling child's soul;

All we can do is sift through the hours

And beg for provision, mercy, and power

To experience life's sentence of lessons and fate

Before we, too, find ourselves in heaven's estate.

Love us and guide us from your ethereal view,

Until one day we are reunited with you.

Being Positive

Does Not Happen

By Chance.

It Is A Decision.

-Diamante Lavendar

Follow Your Heart

Life can be rough.
It can make you want to say,
"Enough is enough! I quit!"

You throw up your hands
In dismay,
Not wanting to go through one more day

Or minute or hour.
But life demands that you keep moving,
Whether you feel motivated or not.

The trials are turbulent.
The road is rocky.
Yet you know you must continue,

Despite your mind screaming
At you
That it's time to quit.

This is the key:
Your mind is not your master.
Your heart discerns your personal truth.

Deep down, you know
That the right thing to do
Is to persevere;

So continue your fight
Until the sun of destiny
Shines on the horizon,

The explanation of all things difficult
Becoming a path of purpose
To heaven's door.

Live your life
With a grateful heart

So that love and goodness
Can transform you.

-Diamante Lavendar

We struggle to understand the effects of grief in our hearts and souls.

It feels like a black, empty void that we are unsure how to fill.

The hardest thing to comprehend is why.

Sometimes we may get an answer to that question, and other times we may not.

It takes a dedicated decision to grow upright into the light of spirit and love

after a consuming loss.

Some of the hardest times during the darkness of
grief are holidays and important markers of celebration for those around us.
While others laugh and rejoice, we want to shut down and give up.
Attitude and perseverance are cultivated in these moments.
Becoming a peaceful warrior is a much healthier stance to adopt
than one of bitterness and victimization.

We are infinite beings.

Our experience on earth

Is merely a

Temporary passage.

-Diamante Lavendar

How can we possibly be happy while the world
celebrates around us? By realizing that
we are all eternal beings with a much greater purpose.
By knowing that earth is a training ground for bigger and better things.

Life

From the dust we are made;
To the dust we return.

In the days of our lives,
Many lessons are learned.

To believe is a key;
To take risks is a cost.

To know true joy and peace,
We must understand loss.

Life indeed is a game
That we must play with care,

And its greatest achievement
Is the love that we share.

To fully understand life, we must understand loss.

To fully live, we must feel not only joy but also pain.

This is a divine plan to enrich us and make us more loving and compatible

with Spirit. Pain forges deep valleys within us. Joy fills those

valleys and brings us back to the mountaintop,

where we can truly say that we live now; we understand both sides of life's story.

Take Time to Know Me

I am here, child;
Take time to know Me.

All of creation
Exists to behold Me.

My essence is found
In the beauty of spring;

I sprinkled the dust
On the butterflies' wings.

I painted the skies
With brushstrokes of blue;

I did this for Me,
And I did this for you.

I made the grass green
Under your feet;

I blessed you with children,
Their kisses so sweet.

I sprinkled stars
In the darkness of night

So you would not fear;
You would still see My light.

I admire your beauty
As you mature and grow;

There's so much I wish for you
And want you to know.

Be still; hear My whisper
In the soft blowing breeze:

"I love you, My precious child;
Take time to know Me."

Those who we are most deeply intertwined with us bless us with
the greatest lessons. We feel the most pain when they leave,
and we feel the brunt of their decisions, good and bad, to our core.
We come to realize that all lessons these people teach us are intricately
important to the betterment of our souls. Those closest to us
give us numerous opportunities for difficult but necessary growth
in the form of forgiveness, empathy, compassion, and the mirror effect.
What we see in these people and don't like very much invariably
are things within ourselves that we need to change.

Waiting

You are my love;
My heart knew you
Before you were born.

Together in another realm we laughed,
Made plans, and shared kisses
As we flew through the endless skies.

My soul mate, my child,
A love so pure and
An innocence undefiled.

Your laugh is a promise
Of truth, beauty,
And a profound future.

To be apart from you
Is like death—but death does not exist;
It is merely a lie of a "three dimensional" world.

Truth prevails and glory remains,
Waiting for me in a realm
That some refuse to believe.

However, I believe. I know.
For I feel angel kisses on my skin,
And I hear the whisper of your voice in the heavens,

Wanting to collect me like a flower,
And bring me home in your embrace,
To my place of refuge where you wait patiently for me.

Life can leave us destined or destitute. The judgment call
is actually up to us more than we may realize.
No, we cannot control the actions of others. We
can only control our own actions. But that is the key!
If we make up our minds to be destined, nothing can hold us back
except our own fears. We might be in rough circumstances,
but the decision is ours whether we thrive or barely survive.

Ghost

I looked for you, but I couldn't find you.
Are you a ghost,
Hidden from what my natural eyes think they see?

I feel you traveling past me,
Somehow all around me,
Yet your touch is not within my reach.

How is it possible
That I sense you? that I know you're there?
Yet there is no evidence.

I'm afraid. I'm confused.
Why is there so much turmoil? so much need for understanding?
Yet the answers I seek come from an invisible realm.

I miss you. I miss how things used to be.
Life was good back then,
Yet I felt back then that I was failing,

Thrashing through throes of waves,
Crashing onto shore,
Where I stood, trying to keep my balance,

I suppose it's time to give up everything I thought I knew
And surrender
To what I believe you're telling me to do.

Please don't lead me astray.
I'm fragile. I'm lost.
I need to know you'll take care of me and that everything will be okay.

When we know we never truly die, that death is only a metamorphosis,
we are free to live happier lives.
The sting of death is only momentary for us. The truth of who we really are
waits for us beyond heaven's veil. There is much more to learn,
much more to see and experience.
Though we mourn those who leave, we find peace and we hope that our
loved ones live on, continuing to inspire us to do our best while we
finish our lives on this planet.

Belief

What you believe does come back to you.

Believe for the best and you will have the best.

Life is like a game: when you learn how to master
the spiritual laws that govern the universe,
you will be mastering the game.

And you have to keep trying until you get it right.

It's a flow of supernatural energy that you succumb to:
it flows in and around you to create your reality.

The truth is, love binds us. It binds us not only on a spiritual level
but also on a soul level. Love is the ultimate force of creation.
That is why our children are so important to us.
We created them (with Spirit's help of course).
When you love someone deeply, you want the best for them
no matter what has happened.
Our loved ones who graduated to heaven still watch over us.
They still pray for us and guide us to the best of their ability.
Death is not an ending but a beginning to a different reality, not only
for the bereaved but also for those who have passed into eternity.

Increase Love's True Grit

For my daughter Celby.
May we all live by her example of love and light.

Be the best you can be;
It's all you can do.
Put yourself in
Another person's shoes.
Restep your reasons,
Your where, and your why;
Only then will you begin to
Grow wings and fly.
Pain is a process,
Letdown a game,
For inside each one of us,
We're all made the same.
Once we embrace this
And dance through our trials,
Life will have meaning;
We'll endure it with smiles.
Heartbreak is a part of
This challenge and course.
If we clear all our hurdles,
We'll break every curse.
So next time a crisis
Of loss and grief hits,
Don't believe the illusion;
Increase love's true grit.

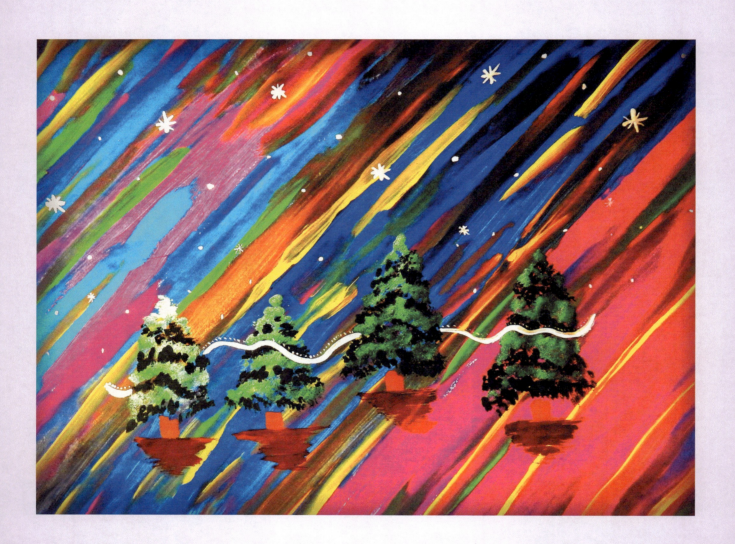

It's all about consciousness. What are you conscious of?

What are you still unconscious about?

What do you believe? What do you want to believe?

Eternal truth can only be found in the silence between the

thoughts that occupy your state of mind and your situation.

Overthinking can be
dangerous.
Try to live by faith.

-Diamante Lavendar

Never Goodbye

You gave me your heart.
I gave you my soul.
Your love and laughter
Made me whole.

Nearly nineteen long years
You graced my life,
Until the reaper came
With sickle and knife.

Your silence is stunning;
Your absence, extreme.
Every second of every day
Is crushing and mean.

My daughter, my love,
The wind in my sails,
Taken from me abruptly,
Snuck through heaven's veil.

How am I expected
To continue living
When all around me
Is pain and misgiving?

In still, ebbing moments,
I remember your voice,
Your laugh, your whisper,
In this deep, numbing void.

That has become
My new sentence to bear;
When all I want
Is to have you back here.

You were everything precious,
A sweet gift from God,
That was ripped from my grasp,
Buried under the sod.

I love you, I break for you,
You're the blood in my veins;
I beg for an answer
To make life seem humane.

But I know oh too well
The truth of this dark place;
I will miss you until
We reunite in God's grace.

Embrace what you've been told is fantasy.

Embrace your imagination of good and love.

Believe in angels. Know that other realms more amazing than you can even imagine do exist.

Hope builds dreams. Hope causes us to climb mountains.

Find what lights your soul on fire and then go for the gusto.

Don't chase you dreams.

Let them overtake you!

-Diamante Lavendar

Everyone's got a dream. And no two dreams are exactly the same.

There's a divine reason for this. You were created for a purpose.

Instead of forcing it to happen, allow Spirit to fill you

with the understanding of what it is.

This will change your life.

Love, mercy, and compassion are the
beautiful backbone of Spirit.
Choose the path of least resistance
and they will become
your way of life.

Now Is All We Have

I am the Method,

I am the Key,

I am the Answer;

Please reference Me.

I am the Creator,

I am the King,

I am the Light

In whom creation sings.

When you're in doubt,

You know you will fall;

Cry out to Me,

The Intention of all.

I am your Redeemer,

Of first and of last.

I am the Gatekeeper

Of all time that does pass.

Sometimes we feel miles away from our purpose
and our destiny.
We're only as far away as we
cause ourselves to be.
Never give up.
Make your destiny your priority.

Peace and Love:
Life's Most
Precious
Commodities.

-Diamante Lavendar

How to Change the World

In order to change the world
you need stamina.

In order to gain stamina
you need to build up your strength.

In order to keep up your strength,
you must have a purpose.

And to have a purpose,
you have to believe.

What is the truth?

We are eternal. We are loved. We are love.

We are works in progress.

Spirit accepts us just as we are, warts and all.

We will have good days and bad days.

At times we will feel grief.

But every illusion will be shattered

when we live according to our dreams.

We will be able to finish well!

To me, peace is an irony.
It's not something
That crept softly
Into my life;
It's something
I had to fight to find.
-Diamante Lavendar

Strength does come from weakness.

Why?

Because we gain strength by overcoming things

we never thought we could handle.

And the bigger your dream,

the more strength you need.

Strong people have overcome many pitfalls.

Strong people don't see pitfalls as disaster!

They see opposition as opportunities!

Life is what you make it.
Will you make lemonade with those lemons,
or will you have a puckered attitude forever?
Hopefully you love lemonade!
And even more hopefully you know that it will taste
much sweeter on the other side!

Afterthoughts

Many say it is folly to follow your heart. They will tell you that you must be level-headed. They will give the wrong advice that you must compete to win. No. This is untruth. In order to "win," you must realize there is no need to win! There is only a need to understand.

We are all on our own journeys. We toil and search to find our way back to where we belong. We hope for a breakthrough. We cling to "someday" and "maybe." We believe that if everything were perfect, then we'd be happy. Another untruth. Happiness is a journey within. It is a place of awakening that, once realized, can be shared with others. Once we have gone through the work leading to enlightenment, we can share in the joy of others who too are enlightened. It is a state of mind.

Heal yourself. Ask Spirit to help. Then others can enter your life to assist your growth. Not until you take the inner journey will you be able to commune in oneness and truth with others.

Know that you are never alone. There are many angels, spirits, and guides who will help you on your path. Believe and you will receive their help. In this process you will accomplish true communion with the Source of love and light.

How do you know when you have achieved this communion? You will be at peace, even in difficult situations.

Remember, life is a journey and we are all works in progress. The goal is unity with Spirit, and the energy of Spirit is love, empathy, compassion, and wisdom.

Until next time, namaste!

I hope and pray that *Finding Hope In The Darkness Of Grief* has blessed you. If you know someone who could use some inspiration, please pass it along.

If I am able to shed light on life's circumstances, even a little bit, I will feel as though I have succeeded with the words and pictures I've put here on paper.

We are all one. We are all intertwined. When one of us finds a step up, it can help others find a step. Heaven on earth is of this concept. Helping each other, enlightening each other, serves a larger purpose.

Thank you for taking the time to invite me into your home and heart. If you enjoyed *Finding Hope in the Darkness of Grief,* please take a moment to leave a review where you purchased a copy. Any help in spreading the word is greatly appreciated!

Sincerely,
Diamante

Diamante Lavendar is the award-winning author of two previously published books.

Diamante's first book, entitled *Breaking the Silence,* has won six awards for inspirational fiction. Based on Diamante's life, *Breaking the Silence* explores issues of abuse, addiction, and loss. *Breaking the Silence* was written to inspire victims of these problems to find hope and healing.

Diamante's second book, *Poetry and Ponderings*, was also written about these topics and includes life insights. *Poetry and Ponderings* has won eight awards for poetry, nonfiction, and inspirational poetry.

Both books can be found on Amazon, at Barnes and Noble, at Kobo, and from Written Dreams Publishing.

If you'd like to connect with Diamante, you can find her on Facebook, Twitter, Google Plus, Pinterest, and (very limitedly) Instagram. Diamante's website can be accessed at www.diamantelavendar.com.

You can find Diamante's award-winning art at www.diamante-lavendar.pixels.com.

Printed in the United States
By Bookmasters